The Grandparents' Little Idea Book

Written and compiled by
Teri Harrison

Published by:
The Grandparent Gift Co., Inc.
Westerville, OH

Distributed by:
Sta-Kris, Inc.
P.O. Box 1131
Marshalltown, IA 50158

Acknowledgments:

Thanks to my husband, Martin, for his belief in pursuing
dreams and his quiet patience. Thanks to my parents,
Art and Ginny, for a childhood filled with a lot of
love, family and friends.- TH

Cover Design By: Warren Hanson
Text By: Teri Harrison
Printed in the United States of America by:
BookCrafters, Chelsea, Michigan
First Printing 1996

ISBN 0-9651801-0-7

Library of Congress Catalog Card Number: 96-94237

Dedication

To my loving grandparents,

Mae Moore
Nell and Arthur Boeker
Delia and Arthur Goehring

*Thank you for the precious
gift of all your "little ideas."*

❋❖❋❖❋❖❋❖❋❖❋❖❋❖❋❖❋

*When a grandchild is born, so too is
a grandparent.
A parent with another chance to touch the
life of a child.*

*And when that happens, what really matters?
Memories- sharing the past, giving time, love
and attention in the present, and leaving
heirlooms for the future.*

*Most memories will be a result of
lots of little ideas.*

*All will be saved in a grandchild's heart
forever.*

❋❖❋❖❋❖❋❖❋❖❋❖❋❖❋❖❋

❖ ❖ ❖ Table Of Contents ❖ ❖ ❖

❖ ❖

❖ ❖ ❖ ❖ ❖ Introduction ❖ ❖ ❖ ❖ ❖

The purpose of this book is to share some "little ideas" with grandparents that can touch the lives of grandchildren. When I think of my grandparents, I think of the silver candy dish on the walnut coffee table in their home. As children, each time my siblings and I visited our grandparents, we raced each other to the covered dish. And whenever we opened the lid, there was *always* something special inside. Though I am well past my childhood years, I will even admit to secretly peeking in the dish on my last visit.

I have come to realize the candy dish was more than *just* a cure for my sweet tooth. It was not only the candy that made me love going to my grandparents' house- it was all the special activities and memorable times I had when I was at my Grandma and Grandpa's. Many of the suggestions shared in this book were my grandparents' "little ideas."

1

Celebrating Grandparenthood

"The love you showered upon your own,
You thought was theirs and theirs alone.
But what a surprise you had in store,
To know that there is so much more."

Welcome To Our Home

Welcome grandkids to your home with a special sign or flag. To make a sign, nail a piece of wood or cardboard to a yard stake. Use stencils to paint a message on the sign like, "Grandkids Welcome Here." For a flag, use a store-bought flag with a design of your choice and call it "the grandkids' flag." If you have more time and creativity, make your own flag out of fabric or felt.

Tell The World

There are many ways to tell the world you are excited to be a new grandparent. Here are a few ideas:

- Place a display or personal ad in a local newspaper.
- Mail birth announcements to your friends.
- Give out candy bars with personalized wrappers that say, "I'm a new grandparent!"
- Put a "new grandparent" sign or banner in your front yard.

Grandparent Newsletters

Subscribe to a grandparent newsletter, such as *Grandparent Times* by Caring Grandparents of America, *Your Grandchild*™ by Trozzolo Resources, or *The Creative Grandparenting Newsletter* by Creative Grandparenting. These wonderful newsletters offer grandparents tips and ideas on how to build and maintain close active relationships with their grandchildren in today's world.

Grandparent Classes

While you are waiting for your new grandchild to arrive, start preparing for your role as a grandparent. Many local hospitals offer specially designed Grandparent classes. If classes are not available or convenient, read current books on childbirth and infant care and consider enrolling in an infant CPR course.

Grandparent's Day

Did you know there is such a holiday?! Each year the second Sunday in September is dedicated to grandparents all around the United States. If possible, make plans to spend Grandparent's Day with your grandkids. Pick an activity and make it an annual family event.

A Grandparent's Club

Start an informal grandparent's club with friends or couples who have grandkids around the same age as yours. Try meeting weekly or monthly for a meal and share stories, pictures, ideas and concerns. Plan an annual event for all club members and their grandkids.

A Grandmother Shower

Host a "grandmother shower" for friends who have their *first* grandchild on the way. Plan the celebration in anticipation of the new baby's birth. If guests want to bring presents, suggest items the baby can use at Grandma's house, or gifts Grandma will need for her new role. Ideal gifts for Grandma may include, a brag book, picture frame, memory book or journal.

Refrigerator Art

Show your grandchildren you appreciate their artwork by posting their handmade cards and drawings on your refrigerator door. When visiting, the kids will be thrilled to see their artwork on display.

Bragging Rights

Showing off the grandkids is not only a joy, but a grandparent's prerogative. Use a pocket photo album to create a brag book with a photo page of each child. In a frame, arrange a collage with grandchildren's pictures. Display the collage on a desk at home or wall at your office.

A Portrait Together

Have a professional portrait taken of you and your grandchildren. If you have just one or two grandkids, consider having a watercolor portrait or charcoal sketch done instead.

Your Silver Candy Dish

Keep a special candy dish or cookie jar at your house filled with treats for the grandkids. It is a good idea to talk with Mom and Dad first about appropriate snacks to offer and limits for the children.

Special Cups

Keep special cups at your house for young grandkids to use when they visit. Use a permanent paint marker to decorate and personalize a few plastic drinking cups just for the kids.

Grandkids' Stuff

Keep items at your home for grandkids to use when they visit. Having your own games, toys and baby necessities, like a highchair or crib, will make visits easier for you and the kids. Many of these items may be things you saved from the time *your* children were young.

Buying Right

Take the guesswork out of finding the best and safest products for grandkids by using reference books or newsletters like, *The Oppenheimer Toy Portfolio* or *The Best TOYS, BOOKS & VIDEOS for Kids.* These resources can help you choose products you and your grandkids will love.

Trash To Treasure!

When your grandkids are ages 1-12, start saving items you would normally throw away: empty egg and milk cartons, toilet paper rolls, coffee cans, old newspapers, magazines and cardboard boxes. Kids will find all kinds of uses for these household items including: school projects, holiday decorations, family gifts, crafts and costumes. Your grandkids will probably turn your trash into treasure!

Many Blessings

Being blessed with many grandchildren can make it difficult to divide your time and attention. However, a tradition of consistent gift-giving can show grandchildren you love them *all* the same. For example, every year you might send $5 bills to grandchildren on their birthdays or give engraved silver cups to newborn grandbabies.

A Garden Of Grandchildren

Start a flower garden as a tribute to your grand-children. Plant a *different* flower upon the birth of each new grandchild. Throughout life, give each child his or her special flower on important occasions. The flower will be a symbol of your love and the child's individuality. Each time a new grandchild enters the world, so too will a beautiful flower.

Great-Grandparents

Great-grandparents have the chance to create happy memories for two generations of children. Consider continuing some of the traditions you began with your grandchildren, with your great-grandchildren. Your adult grandchildren will love seeing their kids treated to many of the *same* traditions they enjoyed as children.

The Other Side

If possible, take the initiative and get to know your grandchild's other set(s) of grandparents. Before a grandchild is born, invite the parent(s) of your daughter-in-law or son-in-law to dinner. After a grandchild is born, send a card or small gift of congratulations to the other grandparents. Keep in touch with them through brief letters or phone calls and add them to your holiday card list. Knowing the other set(s) of grandparents can make celebrations for your grandchild more comfortable and enjoyable for everyone.

2

✱❖✱❖✱❖✱❖✱❖✱❖✱❖✱❖✱❖✱

Welcoming A
New Grandbaby

✱❖✱❖✱❖✱❖✱❖✱

"Hello little grandchild it is me,
My heart's as happy as can be.
I wish for you the sun and moon,
I wish for you a happy tune."

New Baby Bouquet

Make a welcome bouquet for the new baby. Ask your daughter or daughter-in-law if you may dry the flowers she receives in the hospital. Make a bouquet with the flowers and add a pink or blue ribbon. Hang the flowers on the nursery door to commemorate the birth of the new baby.

Baby Time Capsule

Make a time capsule for a newborn grandchild. Save several newspapers and magazines on the day the baby is born. Write the baby a personal letter and store the letter and newspapers in a waterproof box. Seal the box and give it to the child on a future special occasion.

First Tooth & Lock Of Hair

Give parents a place to save baby's first tooth and lock of hair, like a trinket box, frame or lace envelope. Your gift will help preserve two of the most precious souvenirs of babyhood.

Plant A Tree

Give the parents a seedling to plant in honor of the new baby's birth. Mom and Dad may voice concerns over future moves; so, if practical, offer to plant the tree in your yard. As it grows, the tree will become a grand tribute to the child.

The Announcement

Save your grandchildren's birth announcements. Mat and frame the announcements along with each baby's footprints and newborn picture. Display the framed announcements on a wall in your home, and give them to your grandkids when they start families of their own.

Tie A Ribbon

When your grandchild comes home from the hospital, tie a ribbon around the cradle or crib for good luck. Leave the ribbon on the crib to bring good wishes to generations of grandchildren that follow.

Luminary Welcome

Help the family welcome Mom and baby home from the hospital with a beautiful luminary. To make the luminary, put 3-4 inches of sand into the bottom of some brown paper lunch bags. (Make as many bags as needed to spell out the baby's name or date of birth.) In each of the paper bags, stick the bottom of a 6-inch candle about 2-inches into the sand. Arrange the bags on the parents' front lawn and wait until dark to light the candles. The luminary will be a spectacular welcome for Mom and baby.

A Welcome Sign

Make, buy or rent a new baby welcome sign for the proud parents' front yard. Many baby stores carry both pink and blue yard signs and banners that announce the birth of new babies. Contact a company like Stork News, if you want to rent a large personalized welcome sign in the shape of a stork!

Birthstones

At the birth of a grandchild, give the new baby his or her birthstone (see page 133). When the child is older, offer to set the gem in a piece of jewelry, like a ring, necklace, pin or tie tack.

Birth Flowers

Each month has a special birth flower (see page 134). Upon baby's arrival, bring a bouquet of his or her birth flowers to the hospital.

The Language Of Flowers

Make a heartfelt wreath for a new grandchild's room. By consulting a book on the language of flowers, you can select flowers for your wreath that symbolize the goodness of babies: love, hope, purity and innocence. Use dried flowers for a longer lasting wreath and add ribbons, bows, or small wooden cutouts for decoration. The wreath will "speak" a special language from your heart.

Infant Blankets

Give each new grandchild an infant blanket.
These extra-soft blankets, specially made for
infants, are 14-16-inches square and easy to
cuddle and hug.

Bronzed Shoes

Give parents a gift certificate to have their
baby's shoes bronzed. Companies like
American Bronzing, turn baby's first pair of
shoes into a lasting keepsake.

Gifts Of Tradition

Some baby gifts that may seem ordinary *become*
certain future heirlooms. Some of these
traditional gifts are: sterling silver rattles, silver
or pewter cups and spoons, silver banks and
brush and comb sets. Personalize these
treasured gifts by having the child's name and
date of birth engraved.

Baby Hope Chest

Start a baby hope chest for your grandchild.
Traditionally, a hope chest is an accumulation
of clothes and housewares in anticipation of a
marriage. However, you can make a *baby* hope
chest to collect treasures in expectation of life's
milestones. Some of your hope chest items may
include: an outfit for the first birthday, a key
chain for the sixteenth birthday, candles for the
twenty-first birthday and a bottle of champagne
for the wedding night.

Baby Box

A baby box is a place to save baby's mementos.
You can purchase a baby box or make one
yourself. Here are a few ideas:

- ◆ Cover a cardboard box with beautiful baby
  fabric.
- ◆ Build a wooden box or chest.
- ◆ Line and decorate a reconditioned suitcase.

Stencil or engrave the child's name and date of
birth on the top of the baby box.

Letter For The Future

At the arrival of a newborn grandchild, write a letter to the child to be opened and read on an important day in the future, such as graduation or wedding day. Write something you would want the child to know about you, a piece of advice, or just a few words from your heart. Give the letter to the parents to store in the baby's memory box, hope chest or family safe-deposit box. As an adult, the grandchild will truly appreciate the priceless letter from you.

Timeless Treasures

Give your grandchild a cherished gift such as a rocking chair, toy chest or wooden rocking horse. Inscribe or paint the child's name and date of birth on these timeless treasures.

The Nursery

Ask Mom and Dad if you may contribute one special piece of furniture to the baby's nursery. Pass down a family heirloom, or take the parents shopping to help select a gift, such as a changing table, dresser, rocking chair or crib.

The Nursery Nameplate

A nursery nameplate welcomes a new baby. Ask the parents if you may paint or stencil the baby's name on the nursery door or wall; or, for a longer lasting gift, consider giving an engraved silver door-knocker, or an embroidered name plaque.

A Commemoration

Give each new grandchild a commemorative stamp or coin dated with his or her birth year. Your gift will be an enduring token of your love and may be the first stamp or coin in a future collection.

Bib & Diaper Set

Give the baby a matching monogrammed bib and diaper set. Enjoy a bit of whimsy and fun with this gift idea- the bib and diaper will make an adorable outfit for a special photograph.

A Bedtime Tape

If you sing or play a musical instrument, make a lullaby tape for the new baby. If music is not your forte, tape-record a bedtime story instead. A bedtime tape can be a wonderful way to be part of a new baby's life.

A Christening Pin

Give the baby a special pin to wear on christening day, such as a cross, or his or her monogram. Parents can save the pin for the child and it can be worn again on future occasions, such as confirmation or wedding day. The child may also pass down the pin for your great-grandchildren to wear on their christenings.

The Christening Dress

If there is an heirloom christening dress in your family, pass it down to the newest grandchild. Create a family record by stitching each wearer's initials and the christening date at the bottom of the dress. If the dress will be worn again soon, store it in a sturdy box along with a sachet. If the dress will not be worn again in the near future, have it professionally cleaned and boxed.

A Christening Bonnet

Give the baby an heirloom bonnet to wear on christening day. Purchase a new bonnet, sew one yourself, or pass down a family treasure. Many of the christening bonnets available today can become wedding handkerchiefs by snipping a few stitches along the seams. These bonnets make very touching gifts for grandchildren. Like the christening dress, personalize the bonnet with a monogram of the baby's initials and birth date.

Big Brothers & Sisters

When a baby sibling is born, give small gifts to older brothers and sisters. Consider giving activity books designed for new siblings, or shirts or buttons that say, "I'm a Big Sister/ Brother Now". You may also like to throw a new sibling party complete with cake, balloons and party favors.

Sibling Announcements

Help young siblings show their pride and excitement following the birth of a baby brother or sister. Have the siblings hand out bubble gum cigars or illustrate cards announcing their new roles as big brothers or sisters. Make copies of the cards at your local printers, then address and mail the cards to the children's schoolfriends and neighbors.

3

✳❖✳❖✳❖✳❖✳❖✳❖✳❖✳❖✳❖✳

Thinking Of
Mom & Dad

✳❖✳❖✳❖✳❖✳❖✳❖✳

"We were young parents long ago,
Our love and support are yours you know.
We admire and respect the job you do,
And will be there for you two."

Congratulations!

When you hear that your daughter or daughter-in-law is pregnant, send a personal letter or card to the expectant parents. Express your love and support for the parents and your joy and excitement over the news of a new baby.

Safety First

A home safety inspection is a great gift for new parents. Offer to have a professional company, like Safety for Toddlers® show new parents the necessary steps to "baby-proof" their home. If the baby frequently stays at your home, take note of the suggestions, or schedule a safety check for your house as well.

Maternity Wear

Take the mother-to-be shopping for a beautiful maternity dress or nightgown. The expectant mother will appreciate the extra pampering and the time together.

The Shower

Surprise your daughter or daughter-in-law with a sentimental gift at her baby shower. For example, give her a refurbished toy box she or her husband had as a child, a handmade rocking chair, or her favorite childhood stuffed animal.

Helping Hands

Be available for Mom and Dad during the first few weeks of the new baby's life, especially after a difficult birth. An extra pair of loving hands can really make a difference.

Gift Subscriptions

Give the new parents a subscription to a parenting publication. *The Mommy Times*® and *full-time DADS*© are wonderful, unique nation-wide newsletters for parents. *FamilyFun, Parent,* and *Family Circle* are popular monthly magazines for families.

Activity Books

Give new parents a book of activities and projects designed for young children. Check your local bookstore for good titles, or contact a company like The Creative Learning Institute. Subscribers to their publication *Together Time*, receive new kits of wonderful children's activities each month.

A Shadow Box

A shadow box beautifully protects and displays valuable heirlooms. If you saved mementos from the birth of your child, like the hospital band, announcement or first outfit, display them in a shadow box. When your child becomes a parent for the first time, give the shadow box as an expression of delight over the beginning of a new generation. For a special touch, add an engraved nameplate to the base of the shadow box.

A Mother's Charm

Upon the birth of each new child, give Mom a special charm or pendant inscribed with the baby's name and date of birth. Mom will be proud to wear her charms for years to come.

Caring Coupons

Make a gift book for parents with coupons for baby-sitting, video rentals, housekeeping services and local carry-outs. You will show care and concern for Mom and Dad and they can choose when to redeem the coupons.

Parent Love

When you have time alone with the grandkids, help them plan a loving surprise for their parents: bake the parents' favorite dessert, perform a skit with costumes, or prepare a candlelight dinner for the two of them. Parents will be thrilled with the kids' gesture of love.

A Milestone

The first Mother's Day or Father's Day is a milestone for any new parent. Commemorate the day with a gift like:

- ◆ A silver tray engraved with the parent's name, date and a short message.
- ◆ An inspiring poem or quote about parenthood.
- ◆ A cast of the baby's handprint or footprint.

A Night Away

On their anniversary, give parents of young children a prepaid hotel reservation for a night or weekend away. Offer to baby-sit the grandkids. Mom and Dad will get a much needed break and you and the grandkids can have a great time together.

Portrait Surprise

One day, when you have the grandkids all your own, take them for a portrait sitting. Surprise the kids' parents by giving them the portrait on an upcoming wedding anniversary.

Parent Talk

Initiate scheduling a time to talk with both Mom and Dad on a regular basis. Scheduling may be more difficult with step-families or over long distances, but good communication is important for everyone. Discuss upcoming family events and activities, time with grandkids, discipline, caregiving issues, or any other concerns that may arise.

A Message Of Love

Help your grandkids tape a message of love for their parents. Use a tape player or video camera and record the kids reading a poem they have written, singing a special song, or listing the reasons why they think their parents are special. Parents will always treasure their kids' message of love.

4

❈❖❈❖❈❖❈❖❈❖❈❖❈❖❈❖❈

Keeping In
Touch

❈❖❈❖❈❖❈❖❈❖❈

"Grandchild dear I miss you so,
And we're good friends, I truly know.
Although we may be miles apart,
I always have you in my heart."

All-About-You-Book

Making an all-about-you-book is a great idea, particularly for long-distance grandparents of preschoolers. To make the book, use a small photo album, or booklet fashioned from colored construction paper. In the book, include several pictures of yourself and pages full of information: your address, phone number, nickname, birthday, hobbies, pets, etc.. Keep the book simple. Send it to your grandchild and the book will be "read" over and over again. Despite the distance that may separate you from a grandchild, an all-about-you-book can help the child feel closer to you.

Going Home Gift

At the end of a grandchild's visit to your home, hide a small gift or card in the child's suitcase. When the child unpacks the bag and finds your surprise, he or she will be reminded of the special time the two of you spent together.

Let's Make A Deal

Before ending a visit with a grandchild, make a deal to do something together soon. Seal your deal with a handshake. The handshake will establish trust between the two of you and build excitement for the next time you see each other.

An Upcoming Visit

Prepare young grandkids for your upcoming visit. Two weeks before your scheduled arrival, send the kids a package and include:

- ◆ Several recent pictures of yourself.
- ◆ A 2-week countdown calendar that high-lights the day of your arrival (see page 102).
- ◆ Fun stickers the kids can use to mark off the days prior to your arrival.
- ◆ A letter listing some of the things you hope to do together during your visit.

The grandkids will anxiously await your arrival!

"Who's Who?"

Give toddler grandchildren a family photograph of their own. Play "who's who in the family?" by pointing to a person in the photograph, and asking for his or her name and relation. This game can help young children recognize and know family members they rarely see. For slightly older children, make photo flash cards. Glue a picture of each family member on separate 3 x 5 file cards. On the back of each card, write the relative's name, relation and easy-to-remember facts about the relative, such as where he or she lives, career, hobbies, pets, etc.. If possible, have the grandchild "interview" family members to collect information used on the cards. The child may find that using flash cards is an interesting and memorable way of learning about family.

Fax It!

Use a fax to send letters and pictures to your grandkids. In turn, the kids can send *you* letters, short greetings, drawings or handprints- all in a matter of minutes!

Videotapes

Use videotapes to send special messages and wishes to grandkids. In turn, encourage parents to mail *you* tapes of the kids playing around the house and celebrating special events and holidays.

The Hi-Tech Touch

If you and your grandchildren are computer bugs, keep in touch with e-mail messages. It can be fun communicating with a simple push of a button. If you need to learn computer skills, ask your grandchildren for help. They may enjoy teaching their "old" grandparent new tricks.

First Class Love

Keep in touch with grandchildren through the mail. Use a letter writing program to get started, or purchase special stationery, envelopes and stickers that easily identify letters from you. Make sure to save all the letters from the kids and encourage the kids to do the same. It can be fun to read the letters again in the future.

Souvenirs & Postcards

If you travel a lot during the year, keep in touch with grandkids by mailing them postcards or souvenirs. Start a collection of souvenirs for your grandchildren by gathering: T-shirts, magnets, maps, shells, bumper stickers or foreign coins from each trip.

Newspaper Clippings

Stay in touch with adult grandchildren. Clip
cartoons, or newspaper and magazine articles
about each child's career, hobby, or special
interest. Mail the cartoons or articles with short
notes saying, "Just thinking of you."

A Hidden Message

Mail a hidden message to a young grandchild.
Send the child a letter written in white crayon.
Include instructions asking the child to color
over the entire letter with a colored crayon. The
colored crayon will reveal your hidden message.
In return, your grandchild may just mail *you* a
secret message to decode!

A Big Welcome

When meeting grandkids at the bus station or
airport, bring along a big "welcome sign" and a
bunch of brightly-colored balloons. The grandkids will love all the attention!

Ongoing Letters

Begin an ongoing letter series with a grand-child. Here are several ideas to get you started:

◆ Start a story with one or two sentences. Mail the story to your grandchild to continue, then return to you. Keep up the correspondence until, together, you have written a terrific story.

◆ Start your correspondence with the letter A. Draw or clip a picture of an apple and mail it to your grandchild. Ask the child to write back and include a drawing of something beginning with the letter B. See if the two of you can go from A to Z.

◆ Start with the number 1. Draw or clip a picture of one item and mail it to your grandchild. Ask the child to send back a drawing of 2 items and so on- try to count to 100.

Laugh Lines

Trade riddles or jokes with grandchildren through the mail. Send your grandchildren riddles, puzzles, or knock-knock jokes to solve. Ask the grandkids to send jokes or riddles back to you. See how long you and your grandkids can keep up the laughs!

The Mystery Box

Mail your grandchildren a mystery box. Enclose an item in a shoe box, then write down 3-6 clues to its contents. Seal the clues in an envelope and mail the clues along with the mystery box. Your grandchildren will have a great time guessing the contents of the box. Ask the children to call you as soon as they have solved the mystery.

Tell Me A Story

Draw an unusual shape on a blank piece of
paper and send it to a young grandchild. Ask the
child to draw a character from the shape, and
write a story about the character for you. You
will look forward to receiving the child's
imaginative story back in the mail. (Ages 6-10)

A "Special Friend"

Mail your long-distance grandchild a stuffed
animal and attach a letter asking the child to
take care of this "special friend" for you. Ask
the child to write you and tell you how, and
what, the new friend is doing each week.
Through words and drawings, you will get
weekly updates on the "special friend" through
the eyes of your grandchild. (Ages 4-7)

Long-Distance Gifts

Give gift certificates to long-distance grandkids or the entire family. Gift certificates for long-distance phone service, airline tickets, or bus tickets, can make it easier for families to stay in touch.

The First Day Of School

Send a care package to a grandchild as a treat on the first day of school. Ask parents to give your package to the child when he or she arrives home from class. Put the package together your-self or order from a local gift basket company.

A Delicious Welcome

When the grandchildren come for a visit, make it a tradition to cook their favorite dish for dinner on the night they arrive. You will make the grandkids feel special and they will look forward to your delicious ritual!

Moving Away

Mail a welcome package to your grandkids' new home. If you can arrange for the package to arrive before the family does, your gift will provide the first warm welcome. There are many items you can include in the welcome package: homemade cookies, stamps, photographs, a family placard or welcome mat, a phone card or personalized stationery with the new address, etc..

A Picture Together

Give a long-distance grandchild a framed picture of the two of you together. For a young child, use a ceramic frame that reads, "Grandma Loves You" or "Grandpa Loves You." An older child may appreciate a more personal frame. For example, trim a plain frame with items, such as seashells collected on a special vacation, cutouts from old family greeting cards, pieces of heirloom lace, or antique buttons or pins.

5

✽❖✽❖✽❖✽❖✽❖✽❖✽❖✽❖✽

Celebrating

Holidays

✽❖✽❖✽❖✽❖✽❖✽❖✽

"Celebrating holidays is fun to do,
I hope they're happy ones for you.
Creating traditions you'll long remember,
Through the year, January to December."

Holiday History

Share with your grandchildren the history and meaning behind celebrated days. Recount the stories behind each holiday whether it is July Fourth, Passover, Labor Day or Thanksgiving.

Valentine's Day Love

A personally written card or letter that starts, "I love you because...", is a memorable Valentine for a grandchild. Complete the sentence with a list of the child's wonderful qualities. The child will save your written affirmation and read it many times over the years.

Giving Kisses

Give the grandkids a bunch of chocolate kisses for Valentine's Day. Bake peanut butter cookies and top them with chocolate kisses, hold a scavenger hunt for kisses or fill a heart-shaped piñata with chocolate kisses.

Handmade Cards

Help grandkids make personalized cards for holidays like Mother's Day, Father's Day and Valentine's Day. The kids can create their own unique cards for loved ones using construction paper, paints, markers and a decorative die-cut hole punch.

Coupon Books

Create coupon books for your grandchildren. Make the coupons redeemable for small gifts or activities you can do together: popcorn and a movie, a favorite book, a sleepover at your house or a favorite dessert. Make the activities and gifts appropriate for the age of each child. Add the books to Easter baskets or give them with Valentine's Day cards. The coupons will continue the giving long after the holiday is over.

Passover Cookies

During Passover, invite the grandkids over to your house to bake macaroons. Use this special time together to share your childhood memories of Passover.

Easter Bunny Letter

Send a special letter to your grandchild from the Easter Bunny. Companies like Parrish and Brown Printing will mail a personalized letter directly to your grandchild. The child's reaction to the Easter Bunny letter will be worth its weight in gold.

The Perfect Easter Eggs

For Easter, fill plastic eggs with small gifts such as candies, little stuffed ducks or bunnies, crayons or stickers. If you hold an egg hunt at your house, plan a scavenger hunt to find the plastic eggs. If you live far away, the eggs are ideal to send.

Easter Activities

Invite the grandkids over to make Easter crafts.
Here are a few suggestions:

♦   Decorate hard-boiled eggs with dyes,
     crayons, glitter or stickers.
♦   Make Easter bonnets out of paper plates by
     punching holes and stringing ribbons
     through the sides of the plates. Decorate the
     tops of the plates with paper flowers, bows
     and ribbons.
♦   Make Easter baskets from strawberry
     containers or empty milk cartons, decorated
     with paint, crepe paper or construction paper.

A Musical Parade

Help young grandkids plan a July Fourth parade
using homemade musical instruments. Pots and
pans are drums, wooden spoons are drumsticks,
sealed pie tins filled with beans are cymbals,
and combs are harmonicas. The homemade
sounds will be music to your ears!

Fourth Of July Picnic

Hold a family picnic on July Fourth. To plan fun games for grandkids, think back to some of the childhood games you remember playing at fairs and picnics. The grandkids will still enjoy participating in a wheelbarrow race, sack race or egg toss.

Bag Of Halloween Fun

Assemble a fun Halloween treat bag for each grandchild. Try to include items other than candy: novelty pens or pencils, plastic spiders, Silly String, false teeth or mustaches, or Halloween storybooks.

Halloween Seeds

Carving pumpkins at Halloween is a thrill for grandkids, but the seeds are an extra treat. Save the pumpkin seeds to roast and salt (recipe page 130). The seeds are a delicious Halloween tradition *and* much healthier than candy.

"I Am Thankful For..."

Each Thanksgiving, lead your family in giving thanks. Ask everyone in the family to hold hands around the dinner table and name one thing for which they are thankful. If your entire family is unable to be together for the holiday, ask each person to mail a note of thanks. Read the notes at dinner and save them from year to year.

Handmade Place Cards

Have the grandkids make place cards for special family meals. For example, on Thanksgiving, use a black ink pad, and have the grandkids thumbprint a blank place card. Then using magic markers, draw a head, legs and feathers around the thumbprint to create a little turkey. The place cards will decorate your table, and will be tokens of the holiday everyone can take home.

Hanukkah Coins

Give new grandchildren coin books for their first Hanukkah. On following years, hide one collectible coin for each grandchild among some gold *chocolate* coins. The kids' coin books will soon be full of valuable coins and treasured Hanukkah memories.

Dreidl Collection

Give your grandchildren different dreidls every Hanukkah. Encourage the kids to store their dreidls in a special place once the holiday is over. As the years pass, the dreidls will form tangible memories of childhood Hanukkahs.

Hanukkah Recipes

Share your Hanukkah recipes with older grandchildren. If you have special recipes for potato pancakes or Hanukkah cookies, take time to teach your grandkids how to make these celebrated holiday foods.

The Menorah

Give your grandchildren menorahs for their first Hanukkah. The kids can light their own menorahs every holiday season and pass them down to generations that follow.

Grandkids' Gift Exchange

With parents' help, coordinate a holiday gift exchange among the grandkids. Hold a drawing to pick secret pals and suggest the kids exchange handmade presents. Schedule the gift exchange for the week of Hanukkah or Christmas.

A Holiday Game

Start an annual tradition of playing a family game like Yahtzee or Monopoly every holiday season. Rotate a family trophy among the winners and engrave their names on the trophy. Let the winners keep the trophy at their homes until the following year.

Annual Holiday Photo

Every holiday season, take a picture of your grown child's family. Organize the family's picture year-by-year in a holiday album. The album will be a timeline of the family's past. Each year, set out the album where everyone can enjoy it. Your children and grandchildren will love to look at pictures from past holidays, and marvel at how the family has changed.

Christmas Activities

Start a tradition by hosting an annual Christmas activity for your grandkids. Invite the kids to your house to help trim a tree, bake cutout cookies, make ornaments, or decorate gingerbread houses. The kids will definitely look forward to the event each and every year, and may even pass down the tradition to their grandchildren!

Annual Ornaments

Start the tradition of placing a different ornament at each grandchild's place setting on
Christmas Day. One day, when your grandkids
have homes of their own, they will proudly
hang your annual ornaments on their Christmas
trees.

Ornament Box

Give adult grandchildren wonderful boxes to
store and preserve their Christmas ornaments. If
you have given the children Christmas
ornaments over the years, the boxes will be
especially touching gifts.

Keepsake Ornaments

Make Christmas ornaments out of small
souvenirs and keepsakes from the grandkids.
Tie holiday ribbons on the souvenirs and hang
them from your tree every year.

Picture Ornaments

Make a picture ornament of each grandchild. To
make a picture ornament, place a cookie cutter
over a photograph of a grandchild and trace the
outline. Cut out the shape and glue the picture
to the back of the cookie cutter (a star, heart or
diamond shape works well). Using holiday
ribbon, hang the ornament on your Christmas
tree, or string several ornaments along your
mantle or staircase.

The Nativity

Give your grandchild a nativity scene and tell
him or her the story of the first Christmas. A
toddler or preschooler may safely play with a
plastic or fabric nativity set, while an older
grandchild may cherish a wooden or ceramic
nativity.

Advent Calendar

Christmas holds many of our fondest childhood memories. An Advent calendar can focus a child's excitement for the coming holiday, as well as make the 24 days leading up to Christmas just as fun as Christmas Day. Give your grandchild an Advent calendar and put something extra in each pocket or behind each paper door. Include a note for something to do or something to receive each day: a day spent baking, shopping, caroling, or a candy cane, activity book or ornament. The Advent calendar can be a wonderful tradition that marks the start of a glorious holiday season.

The Season For Giving

With grandkids' help, pick a charity to contribute to each Christmas. Together, collect clothing for a local children's home, carol at a senior center, or give a food basket to a needy family. The contributions will remind grandkids that Christmas is the season for giving.

A Handmade Tree Skirt

Make a tree skirt decorated with the grandkids' handprints. Trace the outline of each grandchild's hand on a piece of felt. Cut out the felt prints and sew, or glue them onto a solid-colored tree skirt. Then, if desired, personalize the handprints with the children's names and add any additional decoration. When new grandchildren are born, add their handprints to your tree skirt as well.

Cookies For Santa

Give your grandkids a special plate and mug for Santa's milk and cookies. To make the gift more meaningful, sign your name and date on the back of the plate with a permanent marker or paint pen. Ask Mom and Dad to videotape your grandkids' faces when they see the empty plate and cup on Christmas morning.

A Christmas Eve Tale

Select a favorite Christmas tale to read to your grandkids every year on Christmas Eve. Each year, choose a *different* version of the same story. As the kids learn to read, let them take turns reading the annual tale aloud.

A Tree Of Their Own

Give grandchildren small artificial Christmas trees they can decorate and display in their bedrooms each year. Schedule a day to help younger grandchildren with their decorations. For example, make chains out of popcorn or construction paper, and craft ornaments from old greeting cards, pinecones or baking soda dough (recipe page 130). Every year, the grandkids will look forward to trimming their own trees.

New Year's Eve

If you spend New Year's Eve with young grandkids, make ringing in the new year grand! Spend the early evening hours crafting your own New Year's horns, hats and noisemakers. To make horns, use paper towel rolls decorated with construction paper and glitter. To make hats, decorate paper plates with ribbons, beads and colored markers. For noisemakers, bang pots and pans, or shake coffee cans filled with navy beans. If small children are unable to stay awake until midnight, create your own time to ring in the New Year.

New Year's Day Piñata

Fill a piñata with candies, confetti and small toys. Invite your grandkids over to celebrate New Year's Day with a real bang!

6

✳❖✳❖✳❖✳❖✳❖✳❖✳❖✳❖✳❖✳

Sharing Projects
& Activities

✳❖✳❖✳❖✳❖✳❖✳

"Grandparents are meant for kisses and hugs,
For watching rainbows and catching bugs.
For baking all your favorite things,
For books to read and songs to sing."

Learning Together

If you have a shared interest with an older
grandchild, take a class together. Enroll in a
local community education program or take
private lessons for interests such as computers,
golf or dance.

The Activity Box

Make an activity box filled with fun things to
do each time your grandkids visit. To put
together an activity box, decorate a shoe box
with wrapping paper. Write down activities on
3 x 5 file cards and then put the cards in the
box. Know your grandchildren's interests, so
you can include things they will enjoy doing.
When the grandkids visit, and you do not have
special plans, let them pick a card from the box.
Then do whatever the card says!

Share A Project

Start a project with a grandchild. If you have a
lot of time and energy, consider a large project,
like building a dollhouse, sewing a holiday
outfit or constructing a tree house or fort. For a
smaller project, decorate a T-shirt, assemble a
puzzle, or work on a ready-made craft kit with
instructions and tools included.

"Rainy Day Games"

Keep a supply of "rainy day games" on hand:
dominos, puzzles, pick-up sticks, cards and
checkers. Tic-tac-toe and hangman are great
games to play with just a pencil and paper.

Computer Fun

If you share an interest in computers with a
grandchild, select several computer games you
can play together. Shop computer superstores
for fun educational computer games for kids.

A Day At The Movies

Let your grandchild pick a movie (with an OK
from Mom and Dad), and go to the theater
together. Enjoy popcorn and sodas during the
movie and plan extra time afterwards to share
your thoughts on the film.

The Arts

Invite a grandchild to get dressed up and
accompany you to a play or concert. Make plans
to treat the grandchild to dinner before the
event.

Children's Museums

Find a children's museum in your area and take
the grandkids there for the day. Imagine the fun
you and the kids will have at a place where they
are encouraged to touch everything!

Movies From The Past

Rent a video of one of your favorite movies from the past. Invite older grandkids over to your house to watch the movie with you. Your favorite film from the past may become one of your grandkids' favorites as well.

Write A Book

If a grandchild enjoys writing or drawing, write a book together. Use your imagination to compose a story and illustrations. To create the book, use your own paper and bind the sheets with staples or string, or use a bookmaking kit. Bookmaking kits are available at many children's toy stores or teachers' stores. The kits range from blank hardback books you can write in, to those complete with binding materials, to a mail-in service that professionally typesets and binds your book. If the book is a hit, consider writing a sequel!

Story Time

Spend time together reading to your grand-children. Let the children select their favorite stories and introduce some of the classics you remember reading as a child. As your grand-children learn to read, let them read *you* the stories. Make a point of taking grandkids to storytelling programs held at local libraries or children's bookstores.

Dress-Up Trunk

Kids love to dress up. Purchase a preassembled dress-up trunk, or better yet, design one of your own. To make your own trunk, collect old clothing and accessory items you have around the house, or shop at thrift or consignment stores for interesting and unusual outfits. If you travel a lot, bring home accessories for the trunk as souvenirs. Keep the dress-up trunk at your house for grandkids and great-grandkids to enjoy.

Let's Pretend

Join your grandkids in a game of pretend. Help the kids with costumes and props, and set up a make-believe grocery store, office or school.

Paper Dolls

Make paper dolls for young granddaughters. You can cut paper doll figures from wood, cardboard or plastic milk bottles. To make paper doll clothes, be creative and cut out magazine fashion pictures, or craft outfits from fabric or felt. Attach the doll outfits to the figures with snaps, Velcro, wooden pegs or double-sided tape.

Cardboard Boxes

Cardboard boxes are a surprising source of fun. In a grandchild's imagination, a cardboard box can be a secret fort, race car, pirate ship or dollhouse. Save a few large boxes for a rainy day.

A Silhouette

To make a silhouette of a grandchild, cover a section of wall with poster board or butcher paper. Using a slide projector, cast the child's shadow onto the piece of paper. Trace around the shadow, then cut out the silhouette. Glue the silhouette to a piece of colored construction paper, and give to parents as a delightful surprise.

A Life-Size Self-Portrait

Help your grandchild make a life-size self-portrait. Lay a large piece of butcher paper on a smooth, flat surface. Have the child lie down on the paper and trace the outline of his or her body with a magic marker. Cut out the paper figure. Let the child draw on his or her own features using magic markers, colored pencils, crayons or poster paints.

The Swing

Hang a swing in your yard the grandkids can play on. The swing will provide hours of fun and will likely be a source of many happy childhood memories.

A Scavenger Hunt

Plan a scavenger hunt for your grandkids. If you are entertaining several grandchildren, organize them into teams. Use your home or local park to hide written clues leading to small prizes: packs of gum, rolls of pennies, coloring books, trading cards or crayons. Have the final clue lead to a grand prize that everyone can enjoy, like a trip to a nearby ice cream parlor or skating rink.

Lemonade Here!

Do you remember *your* child's lemonade stand?
A lemonade stand is still a terrific pastime for
kids on hot summer afternoons. Children get an
introduction into the world of exchanging
money and interacting with people, while
adding spare change to their piggy banks. All
you need to provide is a card table, chairs, sign,
lemonade, ice, cups and a little encouragement.
(Do not forget the camera!)

Summer Picnics

Hold a summer picnic at a local park or in your
own backyard. If you have one or two
grandkids, ask them to bring a friend. If you
will have a larger group, you might want some
extra help! Prepare favorite picnic foods and
organize group games. Should bad weather
spoil your plans, have the picnic inside. Spread
blankets on the floor and enjoy (just think-no
bugs)!

Treasure Walks

Take a walk with a grandchild and search for
treasures in your neighborhood or local park.
Make sure to bring along a paper sack, mason
jar, insect net and binoculars. These tools will
help you and your grandchild find and collect
treasures discovered along the way, like giant
pinecones, fuzzy caterpillars and colorful
leaves.

Plant A Seed

Planting a seed, tending it, and watching it grow
is a wonderful activity to share with a grandchild. Whether you have a large garden or a
favorite window box you plant each year, share
the wonder of nature with your grandchild. If
the child lives faraway, send a pack of seeds
and ask the child to keep you up-to-date on the
seed's growth. Suggest the child mail you
drawings or photographs showing the seedlings'
progress.

Feed The Birds

Make a birdhouse or birdfeeder with your grandchild. If you like to work with wood, build a wooden birdhouse. If not, simply roll a pinecone, or empty toilet paper roll, in peanut butter and cover it with birdseed. Put the feeder in a place where you can see the birds eat. Find a book on birds, and with your grandchild's help, identify regular visitors at the feeder.

The Joy Of Fishing

If you like to fish, share the joy of fishing with your grandkids. Take the kids to a local fishing spot and teach them how to bait and cast. Fishing with the grandkids is always fun, even if you do not catch anything!

Athletics

If you are able, play catch, shoot hoops, hit golf
balls or kick soccer balls with your grandkids.
Even a walk around the neighborhood is terrific
exercise, not to mention a chance to spend
quality time with your grandchildren. Physical
activity is great for the minds and bodies of
"kids" of all ages.

Sports Fan

Invite a grandchild to accompany you to a
sporting event. Get tickets for a baseball,
football or basketball game in your area; or,
attend an event of special interest to the two of
you. Together, you will have fun cheering on
your favorite team or player.

The Car

Have a grandchild help you work on your car. If you maintain the car yourself, teach your grandchild the basics of car repair and maintenance. Demonstrate how to refill fluids, check oil and evaluate air in tires. If you do not know a lot about cars, the child can help you wash and wax the car, or pump gas at the filling station.

"Parking Spaces"

If you keep grandkids' bikes or wagons in your garage, or if the kids live close enough to ride bikes to your house, assign each child a special "parking space" in your garage. Use masking tape to section off each space, and put the child's initials on the garage floor. Keep a tire pump, rag and spray bottle nearby so the kids can maintain their own "vehicles." The kids will love it!

Solo Sleepovers

Invite a grandchild over to your house for a solo sleepover. Use blankets to make a tent inside the house, have a camp-out in the backyard, or have a sleeping bag party in front of the television. Your one-on-one time and attention will be rewarding for you and your grandchild.

Attics & Basements

Attics and basements can be magical places for grandkids. Spend a rainy day together going through old treasures in your basement or attic.

Baby Games

Play baby games with a new grandchild. For example, in the first 3 months of life, babies love to play with rattles and mobiles. Babies 6-9 months old love playing patty-cake, peekaboo and this-little-piggy.

Toddler Games

Keep toddlers entertained with games like duck, duck, goose, ring-around-a-rosy and follow-the-leader. If you have forgotten any of these classic games, ask Mom and Dad for a quick refresher.

Toddler Time

Prepare your home to keep toddler grandkids entertained. Here are a few suggestions:

◆ Have plenty of paper, tape, crayons, and play dough (recipe page 131) at your house. Store the toddler supplies in a special plastic tub.
◆ Display alphabet magnets within toddlers' reach on the bottom-half of your refrigerator door.
◆ Store plastic lids, containers and measuring cups in your bottom kitchen cabinet.
◆ Have plenty of picture books and magazines on hand.
◆ Keep cassettes and videotapes of children's songs and programs at your house.

Fun In The Kitchen

Spend a day in the kitchen with your grandkids.
Preschoolers might like to help you bake a
batch of their favorite cookies, while older
grandkids may ask you to help them plan and
cook an entire meal. Keep several children's
cookbooks on hand for these fun days spent
with grandkids.

We Scream For Ice Cream

On a weekend afternoon, invite the whole
family over for scrumptious sundaes. Let the
grandkids help you make great-tasting ice cream
bowls made out of *chocolate* (recipe page 132)!
Scoop ice cream into the edible bowls and serve
a variety of favorite toppings. Everyone will
relish creating their own outrageous desserts.

Let's Go Fly A Kite

On a day when the wind is right, fly a kite with a grandchild. You will both enjoy the challenge of getting your kite in the air and the excitement of seeing it fly!

Tea Parties

Do you have fond memories of a tea set you owned as a child? Give your granddaughter a tea set she can play with and save as a keepsake. Let your granddaughter invite you to a tea party; or, if you enjoy throwing parties, plan one of your own. Send invitations to Moms and Granddaughters requesting "dressy" attire. Set your dining table with good china, linens and flowers. Serve tea, finger sandwiches, cakes and cookies. Afterward, send everyone home with a party favor. For a larger event, invite other friends to participate with their daughters and granddaughters. If the tea party is a smashing success, schedule one every year.

Vacationing With Grandkids

If it is possible to travel with your grandkids, plan a vacation together- a day outing, weekend, week or more. Schedule your own itinerary or use a company like Grandtravel, that offers special vacation packages for grandkids and their grandparents. If planning your own schedule, get maps and guidebooks from the library, bookstore or AAA. Invite the grandkids over to your house to help you plan the trip. Ask each child to research a different state or city along your route. Each child can then act as the "official tour guide" when the group visits his or her assigned area.

One Dirty Day

If you are adventuresome, really get dirty with the grandkids. Join the kids when they make mud or sand pies or spend a warm rainy day (without thunder and lightning!) playing outside.

The First Of Spring

On one of the first nice days of spring, spend
the day outdoors with your grandkids. Entertain
preschoolers by blowing bubbles and drawing
with colored chalk on the sidewalk. Older kids
may want to ride their bikes, roller skate, jump
rope or play hide-and-seek.

Lazy Days

On days too hot to do anything- do nothing!
Grab a cold glass of lemonade and spend the
day with a grandchild. Together, sit underneath
a cool shade tree or lie in a backyard hammock.

A Snowman Family

When the ground is covered with snow, spend a
day helping grandkids build a snowman family.
Suggest the grandkids dress the snowmen to
resemble members of their family. When the
snowmen are complete, invite Mom and Dad to
take pictures for the family album.

7

✳❖✳❖✳❖✳❖✳❖✳✳❖✳❖✳❖✳

Giving Time,

Love & Support

✳❖✳❖✳❖✳❖✳❖✳

"A grandparent gives so many things,
Hugs, hands, cheers and wings.
Be happy, have fun with this new role,
Share your time, your heart, your soul."

The Joy Of Helping Others

Share with your grandkids the joy of helping others. Collect canned goods together and donate them to a local shelter; or, have the kids help you gather a donation for The Salvation Army or Goodwill. If you are a member of a charitable organization, take advantage of opportunities to include the grandkids in fundraising activities.

Acts Of Love & Kindness

Let your grandchildren see you practice acts of love and kindness. Whether working at your church, helping an ill neighbor, or donating money to a worthy cause, these deeds of kindness toward others will be lasting examples for your grandkids.

Lend An Ear

Take time to listen to your grandchildren. When they talk to you, try to give them your full attention. Listening is a gift your grandchildren will always remember.

"Words Of Love"

One of the greatest gifts you can give your grandkids every day, without fear of spoiling, is words of love, praise and encouragement. Give these "words of love" freely and often.

Being There

Attend grandkids' sporting events, recitals, plays and open houses when you can. Grandkids will glow with delight when they see you and your video camera!

"I'm Sorry"

If you know one of your grandchildren has hurt a sibling or exchanged harsh words with a parent, help the child learn to say "I'm sorry." Encourage the child to make an apology card or talk directly to the person who was hurt.

The "Feel Better Box"

When grandkids are not well, whether they are sick, sad, or miss absent parents, let them play in your "feel better box." Decorate a shoe box with cheery wrapping paper, then fill it with little toys and treasures: small toys collected as giveaways, coins, interesting rocks or seashells. When your grandchildren need to feel better, they will look forward to exploring in your "feel better box."

Love & Concern

Little things can mean a lot to a seriously ill grandchild. Show your love and concern for the child by sending or delivering a small gift every few days, such as a funny card, book, pad of writing paper, flower or photograph. If the child is bedridden, offer to help parents or siblings decorate the bedroom.

A "Comfort Gift"

Give an ill or troubled grandchild a "comfort gift" as a reminder of your constant love. A young grandchild may appreciate a blanket or stuffed animal. An older grandchild may find comfort in a lucky rabbit's foot, locket or photograph. A "comfort gift" can make a child feel better, despite difficult times.

Fixing Boo-Boos

Fix your grandchild's minor bumps and bruises
with a little care and a lot of love. Keep a
supply of children's Band-Aids at your house.
When you need to use a hot or cold compress,
disguise it as a lovable stuffed animal. Insert a
hot-water bottle or ice pack into a pair of
children or adult animal slippers. In no time, the
child's tears will turn to smiles.

A Grandchild's Talent

Every grandchild has a talent. Take special
interest in a child's talent and encourage him or
her to pursue it. Share books on the subject, and
offer to attend educational programs or events
with the child. Give gift certificates toward
lessons or needed equipment such as skates,
easels, paints or tools.

Working Grandparents

Let your grandkids see you at work. Busy career grandparents can take older grandkids to work for a short visit, or even an entire day. Use this time together to reinforce the value of work and discuss the child's career aspirations. If you own your own business, consider hiring the grandchild to do small jobs, like emptying the trash, filing or cleaning.

Teaching & Learning

Take advantage of opportunities to teach your grandchildren new skills. For young grandkids, a skill might be as simple as making a bed, grilling a cheese sandwich, or using a telephone. For older grandkids, consider sharing a talent such as sewing, woodworking, painting or playing a musical instrument. In return, ask your grandchildren to teach *you* new skills. Perhaps you will learn a new dance or how to use the latest computer program.

Pet Names

Invent a loving pet name for a young grandchild, like "Angel", "Princess" or "Little
Buddy." The child will enjoy having a special
name, and it can be a nice way to show your
love and affection.

A Secret Spot

Have a secret spot for you and a grandchild to
meet. Pick a tree or bench at the park, or a
certain room in your house. Consider the spot a
special place just for the two of you.

Milk & Cookies Time

Set aside a time each month to have milk and
cookies with a young grandchild. Spend your
time together talking and sharing. If possible,
when the grandchild becomes an adult, continue
your ritual over a cup of tea, coffee or milk.

A Special Style Of Love

Invent a special sign of love you use only with your grandkids. Be creative and ask the kids for suggestions. Perhaps they want to have a secret handshake, a wink of an eye, tug of an ear, or a big bear hug and cheer. End every visit together with a special style of love.

Hand In Hand

Start a family tradition of holding hands and giving thanks at special mealtimes. Even if your religious beliefs differ, a group prayer, moment of silence, poem or joint hand squeeze can bring everyone a little closer.

Say It With Flowers

Send flowers to an adult grandchild. A floral arrangement or bouquet is a lovely gift for an older grandchild who has moved into a new house, landed a big job, or received a prestigious award.

"I Care Notes"

Surprise grandchildren with "I care notes." Ask Mom and Dad to put the caring notes into the grandkids' lunch boxes or schoolbags. Your "I care notes" can include words of encouragement before final exams, or funny jokes or sayings to brighten gloomy days.

The Family Walk

After a big family meal, go for a group walk. Get your entire group together, whether it is 4 or 40. The walk could be a fun tradition and possibly a neighborhood event- depending on the size of your family!

A Phone Call Away

Give grandchildren prepaid phone cards to call you in emergencies. If the children cannot reach their parents, or if they find themselves in dangerous situations, the phone cards can be real lifesavers.

Tools For Education

Help make sure your grandkids have the tools necessary to achieve in school. Good gifts will always include items that encourage learning, like books, encyclopedias, science kits and calculators. If you have the financial resources, you may even consider opening a savings account or trust to help pay for your grand-children's college education.

A Little Bit More

If your grandkids have dual-working parents or live in a single-parent home, volunteer to serve extra-duty. If you have time, ask parents if you can help by joining the PTA, or serving as a room mother, Boy Scout Leader or Little League coach.

A Shoulder To Lean On

Be available to help your grandkids cope with difficult family situations like death and divorce. Two excellent resource books for grandparents are: *Helping Your Grandchildren Through Their Parents' Divorce*, and *Grandparent Power! How to Strengthen the Vital Connection Among Grandparents, Parents and Children.* If you need information about raising grandchildren, contact the AARP's Grandparent Information Center for additional information and support.

8

✳❖✳❖✳❖✳❖✳❖✳❖✳❖✳❖✳❖✳

Celebrating
Special Days

✳❖✳❖✳❖✳❖✳❖✳

"Birthdays and weddings are just a few,
Of special days that will come to you.
We'll have days packed full of fun,
We'll enjoy them one-by-one."

Birthday Dinners

Take your grandchildren out to dinner for their birthdays. Let each child choose the restaurant and go as your guest of honor. Although birthday parties are fun, children with brothers and sisters can yearn for more personal time with their parents and grandparents. Birthday dinners are an excellent way to give grandchildren extra time and attention.

Birthday Dollars

If possible, give your grandchildren annual birthday dollars to save in their own banks. Consider giving the dollars, along with piggy banks, for the children's first birthdays. On following birthdays, try presenting the dollars inside blown-up balloons or plastic golden eggs. Children can learn a great deal about spending and saving by having a little money of their own.

Birthday Box

When you are unable to be with a grandchild on his or her birthday, send a birthday box including party hats and favors, balloons, a disposable camera and birthday present. Ask Mom and Dad to take pictures at the party with the disposable camera, and then return the camera to you.

Growth Candles

Give your grandchildren growth candles for their first birthdays. The special candles have lines that mark each year of growth, up to age 18. To celebrate each birthday, light the growth candles in a family ceremony and let the candles burn down to next year's mark.

Birthday Tablecloth

Each year, provide a paper tablecloth for your grandchild's party guests to autograph. Give each guest a colored pen to sign the tablecloth, or to write a special message to the birthday boy or girl. Having an autographed tablecloth can become a fun party tradition.

A Birthday Treasure Hunt

Sometime during a grandchild's birthday week, invite the child over to your house for a treasure hunt. Hide clues around your house that lead to small treasures, like cupcakes, balloons, coins or cards. Save the birthday present for the final clue. This birthday event is sure to be a treasure!

A Birthday Memory Book

Start a birthday memory book on your grand-child's first birthday. Use a blank journal or scrapbook, and record the party guests, gifts, games, party favors, cake, and other important or interesting information from the day. Include several photographs in the book as well. Give the book to Mom and Dad so they can record the child's future birthday memories.

Annual Birthday Letter

Write an annual birthday letter to each of your grandchildren. Tell the children many of the things they have done over the past year, how they have grown, time you have spent together, and your wish for them over the coming year. The letter will be easier to do if you keep a notebook or journal throughout the year.

Birthday Shopping Trip

Schedule a birthday shopping trip with a teen-age grandchild. Treat the teen to lunch or dinner, followed by a shopping trip for his or her present. Specify how much you will spend for a gift and leave the selection up to the teen.

Birthday Flags

Give your grandkids birthday flags to fly during their birthday week. Make or buy birthday flags, then personalize the flags with felt or cloth cutouts that reflect each child's personality, hobbies and interests.

Cherished Wedding Gift

On a grandchild's wedding day, give the couple something of yours the grandchild cherished from his or her childhood, like an old toy chest, locket or photo. As an adult, your grandchild will appreciate the gift and the sentiments it holds- your love, joy and happiness.

Something Old

When a grandchild marries, give the bride something you carried or wore on your wedding day, such as a garter, handkerchief, veil or Bible. Passing on a memento from your wedding can link the past to the present.

A Wedding Wish

Write a personal letter or poem to the wedding couple expressing your wishes for their marriage. Read the letter at the wedding ceremony or reception, and later give the letter to the couple to save. Your grandchild and his or her new spouse will cherish your wedding wish.

Wedding Day Tribute

Help assemble a special collection of photos of the wedding couple as babies, youngsters, teens and adults. On the wedding day, present the photos in an album or, with some help, plan a short slide show for the reception.

The First Home

When an adult grandchild moves into his or her
first home, give the child a heartwarming
welcome gift. Here are a few suggestions:

◆ Give flowers from your garden that can be
  replanted in the child's garden.
◆ Make a welcome mat, wreath or name
  plaque for the front door.
◆ Give a basket filled with small gardening
  tools and flower or vegetable seed packs.
◆ Enlarge and frame a picture of the new
  house.

School Years Frame

Give your grandchild a school years frame on
the first day of school. Available in many
department stores, the frame has 12 spaces, one
for each year's school picture. You may consider buying two frames- one for the child and
one for display in your home!

The First Day Of School

Ask Mom and Dad if you can contribute to the first day of school each year. If the parents buy new outfits for the kids, maybe you can add a lunch box, backpack or school supplies.

The First Snow

Celebrate the first snowfall with grandkids, by making a batch of delicious homemade snow ice cream (recipe page 131). Make the snow ice cream more tasty with toppings like cherries, nuts, chocolate chips and sprinkles.

Theme Dinners

If possible, plan time for family dinners on a regular basis. Try creating themes for each meal like "Italian Night", "Hawaiian Night" or "Southern Cooking Night." When the grandkids are old enough, let them select the menus and decorations.

"Grandkids Only" Party

If you have quite a few grandkids, plan a "Grandkids Only" Party. With parents' help, select a date and send the kids invitations requesting "party" attire. Serve cake and ice cream and plan some fun games and activities. Take Polaroid pictures of the kids during the festivities. For souvenirs, send the kids home with their pictures set in inexpensive frames.

Countdown Calendars

Make a countdown calendar for grandkids who are excited about an upcoming event, such as a birthday, vacation or the first day of school. To make a countdown calendar, copy the month's calendar onto a large piece of constrution paper or poster board. As each day passes, instruct the kids to mark an "X" through that day. Creating fun countdown calendars for any anticipated day, let's kids see *the day* approaching, and makes the waiting more enjoyable for everyone.

Family Reunions

Plan a family trip or reunion every year or two. If everyone lives fairly close, meet at a park or local attraction. If you have family across the country, choose a central location. Plan a daylong event, weekend or week's vacation for the family. Take a lot of pictures and bring photo albums to share from past trips. Arrange activities and games for the kids such as skits, crafts, softball, volleyball or miniature golf. If vacationing for a week, assign each family a group meal to plan and prepare. Encourage the families to come up with themes for the meals and include decorations and entertainment. For more ideas, read *Reunions Magazine* which offers all kinds of information for organizing successful reunions.

Declare It A Holiday!

Pick a day when you are going to be with a grandchild and declare it a holiday. Celebrate the day together any way you wish!

Mother & Daughter Days

Plan a special time for Grandmas, Moms and Granddaughters to be together. Plan a luncheon, a daylong shopping excursion or a weekend away. Share family stories and record your time together with pictures and a journal. If everyone agrees, make your time together an annual event.

Father & Son Days

Plan a special time for Grandpas, Dads and Grandsons to be together. Choose a day or weekend for your event. Enjoy playing games, watching sports, feasting or just clowning around. Remember to take pictures of your time together.

9

✳❖✳❖✳❖✳❖✳❖✳❖✳❖✳❖✳

Saving & Sharing

Memories

✳❖✳❖✳❖✳❖✳❖✳

"I hope that many years from now,
You'll look back and feel quite proud.
To have the memories I've shared with you,
The past, the present, the old and new."

Your Story

Record the story of your life! Although many of your life's events may seem ordinary to you, they can be of great interest to your grandchildren and your entire family. There are many different ways to record your personal history, but here are a few suggestions:

- Complete a personal history book or tape program available in many bookstores.
- Talk into a tape recorder and recount many of your life stories.
- Dictate your memoirs to a family member.
- Hire a professional company that specializes in making life story videos.
- Write out your memories longhand, or use a computer.

Select the best approach for you, but take the time to record your stories and pass them on to your grandchildren. Your memories are a gift only *you* can give- *they will be treasures.*

A Grandparent's Journal

Keep your own journal to capture important details of your grandkid's lives. Purchase a grandparent's journal or scrapbook where you can record family trips and holiday events, save grandkids' pictures and mementos, and keep notes of heirlooms and special gifts.

A Memory Box

Everyone needs a memory box- a special place to keep personal treasures. Take a day and share some of the mementos in your memory box with your grandchildren. Tell the kids the stories behind many of the things you have saved and help the kids start memory boxes of their own.

Old Family Photos

Make copies of old treasured family photos and pass them on to your kids and grandkids. The photos will give a perspective of time, and a record of the history of your family.

A Trip Down Memory Lane

Take your grandchildren on a trip down memory lane. Visit the town where you grew up or spent time as a student or young adult. Point out where you went to school, the church where you married, or your first house or apartment. Show the kids the town landmarks (or where they used to be)! If possible, visit some of the people who were part of your life at that time.

Your Most Famous Recipe

Teach older grandkids how to make your most famous recipe, whether it is your to-die-for apple pie, outrageous chocolate chip cookies, or famous macaroni and cheese. The next time you plan to make the recipe, show your grandchildren how they *too* can make a beloved family favorite.

Family Recipes

Record your favorite family recipes in a journal or recipe book. Give copies of the book to older grandkids, or your own grown children, as a Christmas, Hanukkah or wedding gift. If you want to make the book a family project, ask relatives to contribute their best recipes, and print a family cookbook. Companies like Cookbook Publishers, Inc., offer families affordable opportunities to self-publish personalized family cookbooks. Your family will love knowing how to make famous family dishes, and everyone will have the time-honored recipes for future generations.

Your Favorite Game

Share your favorite childhood game with your grandkids. What was the game? How was it played? Who did you play it with? If it is some-thing you can do together, show the grandkids how to play.

Your Favorite Songs

Teach your grandkids some of your favorite childhood songs- perhaps the songs are still popular today. If not, teach your grandkids the words and sing the songs together often.

Wit & Wisdom

Keep a notebook of special quotes and sayings that express your sentiments as a grandparent, and your philosophy of life, love and work. Gather the quotes over time and give them as treasured gifts to adult grandchildren.

Generations Portrait

If your family is fortunate enough to have several generations living, arrange a professional portrait setting to include great-grandparents, grandparents, parents and children. Make copies of the prized portrait for all the families to proudly display in their homes.

On The Day You Were Born

If you did not have the opportunity to put together a time capsule on the day your grand-child was born- it is not too late. Go to your local library and look-up magazine and newspaper articles written on the day the child was born. Make photocopies of the most interesting and important events of the day and arrange the copies in a 3-ring binder or scrapbook. The scrapbook will be a valued gift you can give to a grandchild of any age.

Heritage & Customs

Pass on your family's ethnic and cultural heritage to your grandkids. Share the dress, food, rituals and customs unique to your culture. For special holidays, give your grandchildren gifts significant to your heritage.

Daily Journal

Encourage your grandchild to keep a daily diary or journal. Let the child know that a journal is a terrific way to begin telling his or her life story.

A Family Calendar

Involve the whole family in the creation of an annual calendar. Equally divide the 12 months of the year among family members. For each month(s) assigned, the person or family is responsible for filling in the holidays and creating artwork to decorate the top of that month's page. Complete the calendar by passing it to each family so they can fill in their own birthdays, vacations, anniversaries, weddings, graduations, etc.. Make copies and bind the calendars. Give a calendar to each family at the start of the new year. Having a family calendar will ensure special days will not go unnoticed!

Family Trees

Help your grandchildren learn about the relatives that make-up your family tree. Here are a few suggestions:

◆ Use your computer to generate a simple family tree, or to create a detailed ancestral chart. Use a good computer software program like *Family Ties,* to make the project easier.

◆ Draw a tree with several branches on a large piece of poster board. Cut out large leaves from construction paper. On each leaf put: a photo, the family member's name, relation, and one easy-to-remember trait. (For example: Aunt Jane loves cats.) Organize the leaves on the tree, then display the tree where the kids can play with it.

◆ Organize a family photo album or 3-ring binder. Dedicate one page to each family member include: a recent photograph, name, relation and other important information.

113

Family Time Capsule

Organize a time capsule for the entire family. Have each family member collect 3 or 4 personal mementos and write a letter addressed to future generations. Put the letters and mementos in a large sturdy waterproof container and seal it carefully. When the future generation opens your time capsule, 50 or 100 years from now, they will get a glimpse of the lives of their ancestors.

Memories Of Your Home

Although many of us have memories of Grandma and Grandpa's house, it would be nice to have an actual record of the visits. Keep a blank journal or guest book at your home and each time the grandkids visit, have them briefly write in the book. The kids can write how they spent the day, or if they are too young to write, they can draw pictures. Save the journal and give it to the grandkids to enjoy as adults.

Grandchild's Keepsake Box

Start a keepsake box for each grandchild, as an easier alternative to a scrapbook or baby book. Save letters, cards and handmade gifts from each grandchild, and store them in a special keepsake box. Use a cardboard box, photo storage box or wooden box, and file the mementos in chronological order. Share each grandchild's box with him or her on a special day in the future.

The Funniest Things

Grandparents are famous for recounting the funny things kids say and do. Keep a notebook handy to record your grandkids' escapades and adorable sayings. Make a copy of your notebook for Mom and Dad; they will find its contents just as precious as you do.

All-About-Me-Poster

Help a grandchild make an all-about-me poster
for his or her bedroom. With a marker, divide a
piece of poster board into eight sections. Title
the sections: me, my family, my friends, my
pets, my school, my favorite things, my talents,
my dreams. Fill in the each of the squares with
the child's information, then have the child add
drawings and photographs. Make a new all-
about-me-poster every school year. (Do not
forget to save the old ones.)

Handprints & Footprints

Each year ask the grandkids to make a set of
lasting handprints and footprints for you. For
handprints, use non-toxic paint or plaster of
paris. Pen each child's name and date on the
back of the handprints and display them in a
cabinet or on a wall. To make footprints, cast
the kids' footprints in concrete and use as
stepping stones in a garden or patio.

10

✳❖✳❖✳❖✳❖✳❖✳❖✳❖✳❖✳

Giving Gifts From The Heart

✳❖✳❖✳❖✳❖✳❖✳

"Now they may seem like little things,
But in time, they'll be gifts of kings.
Of all the presents throughout the years,
It's the little things you'll hold most dear."

It's The Little Things

Even small gifts can become great treasures.
Grandpa's old yo-yo or Grandma's lace hankie
may be gifts of a lifetime. Do not overlook the
little things that mean a lot.

"You're The Best" Plate

Use a "You're The Best" plate to recognize a
grandchild's success. A child will feel honored
when recognized with the plate at a family meal.
Find a solid-colored ceramic plate you can
personalize with a paint pen. Stencil in large
letters, "You're The Best" or a similar message.
Use the special plate when a grandchild earns a
high test score, hits a home run or helps a friend
in need. Log the child's name, date and
achievement on the back of the plate with the
paint pen. The plate will be a lasting record of
your grandchild's accomplishments.

Charm Bracelet

Give a charm bracelet to a granddaughter. On future special occasions, give her charms for the bracelet that reflect her interests, hobbies and personality. Your granddaughter will be excited each time she receives another charm from you.

Add A Pearl

Give a young granddaughter a single-pearl necklace. On future holidays, give her pearls to add to the necklace. By the time your granddaughter is an adult, she will have a splendid heirloom from you.

A Train Set

Give a train set to a young grandson. Over several years, use special occasions to present your grandson with pieces to the train set. As a boy, your grandson will have a wonderful train to play with, and as an adult, he will be able to share the train with *his* children.

Collections

Encourage your grandkids to start collections of their own, like coins, stamps, baseball cards, or dolls. The children will love talking to you about their collections, and you will have an easy time giving gifts you know they will love.

A Growth Chart

A growth chart is a terrific gift for a young grandchild. You can purchase a growth chart or make one from wood, cloth, felt or construction paper. On the child's birthday each year, hold a family "measuring" ceremony. Have the child stand next to the chart and mark the new height. The whole family will enjoy seeing how much the child has grown over the course of a year.

Surprise Baskets

Assemble a surprise basket for the grandkids, or even the entire family. Fill the basket with gifts like favorite baked goods, fresh fruits, craft supplies, small toys or family games. Give the basket for *no special reason!*

Personalized Cards

Finding appropriate greeting cards for older grandkids can be difficult. Start a tradition of purchasing blank cards and writing personal messages inside. The cards will have more meaning for you and your grandkids.

Gift Certificates

Give those "hard-to-buy-for" teenage grand-children gift certificates for activities or items they may enjoy. Popular places to buy gift certificates: movie theaters, malls, record stores, skating rinks or fast-food restaurants.

College Care Pack

Send a care package to a grandchild bound for college. Arrange for the package to arrive the first week of school. Include in your care pack: homemade cookies, snacks, stamps, stationery, rolls of quarters and laundry detergent!

Travel Grab Bags

Make travel grab bags for grandkids to enjoy on family vacation. In each grandchild's bag put several small gifts: travel games, pens, pencils, sticker books, packs of gum or snacks. Before the trip, ask Mom and Dad to select landmarks along the vacation route, where the kids can pick an item from their bags. The kids (and Mom and Dad) will enjoy the grab bags, and find long trips easier to manage.

A Vacation Record

Give your grandchild a travel journal and disposable camera to take on vacation. If vacationing near water, give the child an underwater disposable camera. If heading to the desert or mountains, a panoramic camera would be ideal. The journal and camera will provide the child with hours of fun and unforgettable vacation memories.

Family Reunion Souvenirs

Order special souvenirs to give out to everyone attending your family reunion. Ask a creative family member to create a unique design, or let the grandkids invent a family logo. Use the design or logo to personalize souvenirs, such as T-shirts, sweatshirts, baseball caps or buttons.

Kids' Subscriptions

Give your grandkids subscriptions to children's magazines, like *Highlights for Children*, *Boy's Life*, *Your Big Backyard*, *Ladybug*® or *Sports Illustrated for Kids*. These publications are packed with fun and learning and the grandkids will love receiving mail addressed to them!

Personalized Books

Give young grandchildren personalized storybooks. There are several children's book companies who add children's names (and yours too) to the text of a number of storybooks. It is thrilling for kids to see their names in print and themselves as characters in their favorite stories.

And More Books...

Good books are always great gifts for grand-kids. Look for classic titles, as well as recommended new books. Soft fabric books and cardboard books are great for toddlers'. Preschoolers enjoy illustrated and interactive books, while older children may enjoy reading a book series. If you do not live near a children's bookstore, join a book club. If you saved any of *your* children's books, share them with your grandkids. You might even consider combining the old and new books to create a "library" for your grandchildren and great-grandchildren.

Memorable Outfits

If you sew, make young grandkids memorable outfits. For example, make matching pajamas for a granddaughter and her favorite doll, or sew an action hero costume for a young grandson. As children, the kids will love to wear the outfits; as adults, they will fondly remember the special garments.

Special Quilt

Give your grandchild a special quilt as a gift on a graduation or wedding day. To make the quilt, use fabric befitting the occasion, or swatches from clothing the grandchild wore during his or her childhood. Another option is to purchase a quilt, or have one made for you from the material you selected.

Grandpa's Favorite Shirt

Turn one of Grandpa's gently worn dress shirts into a play outfit for a grandchild. If you sew, make a toddler a one-piece romper. If you do not sew, give the shirt to an older grandchild to use for arts and crafts. Personalize the shirt with the child's initials. If Grandpa is willing, suggest he and his grandchild wear matching shirts!

Chef's Hat & Apron

If a grandchild loves to help you in the kitchen, make him or her a special chef's hat and apron. Decorate the apron and hat with fabric paint or an iron-on decal. Keep the pair at your house for the child to wear when you work in the kitchen together. For fun, you might like to make yourself a matching apron and hat as well!

A Sleepover Tote

If your grandkids frequently stay with you, give them sleepover totes for their clothes and toys. Use plain canvas totes and personalize them using fabric paint. As an extra touch, add iron-on decals or sayings such as "Going to Grandma's" or "My Special Bag for Grandma and Grandpa's."

A Tooth Fairy Pillow

Give your grandchild a tooth fairy pillow. You can purchase a tooth fairy pillow or make one yourself. Here are a few suggestions:

◆ Stitch a small pocket for the tooth on the chest of a favorite stuffed animal.

◆ Make a lace pillow with a pocket in the center for the lost tooth. Present the pillow in a box for safekeeping. The pillow may also be used as a wedding ring pillow in the future.

◆ Make a drawstring pouch out of colorful fabric. Add the child's name to the pouch using stencils or iron-on letters. Include a file card in the pouch to record the date of each lost tooth.

11

❋❖❋❖❋❖❋❖❋❖❋❖❋❖❋❖❋

Recipes

&

Resources

❋❖❋❖❋❖❋❖❋❖❋

Recipes

Pumpkin Seeds

- ◆ Remove seeds from pumpkin and clean thoroughly.
- ◆ Preheat oven to 300 degrees.
- ◆ Oil baking sheet or lightly coat seeds with margarine.
- ◆ Bake seeds for 25 minutes or until crunchy.
- ◆ Lightly dust with salt and serve!

Baking Soda Ornaments

- ◆ Mix together: 2 cups baking soda
             1 cup cornstarch
- ◆ Add to mix: 1¼ cups water
- ◆ Cook mix over medium heat. Stir constantly until mix is consistency of mashed potatoes.
- ◆ When mix is cool enough to handle, roll-out to ¼ inch thick.
- ◆ Cut dough with cookie cutters. Press hole in top with toothpick to insert hanger.
- ◆ Allow to dry flat overnight. Decorate with paint, permanent markers and glaze.

Play Dough

- Mix together: 2 cups flour, 1 cup salt
  4 teaspoons cream of tartar
- Add to mix: 2 cups tap water
  3-4 teaspoons food coloring
- Cook mix over medium heat and stir for 4-5 minutes.
- Remove from heat and let stand for 5 minutes.
- Knead dough for 30 seconds until blended.
- Store dough in airtight container.

Snow Ice Cream

- Gather clean, newly fallen snow in large pot.
- Mix milk and vanilla together.
- Sprinkle layers of sugar between layers of snow.
- Fold in milk and vanilla mixture- mix gently.
- Eat ice cream right away!
  Note: Snow ice cream needs to be made by taste, there are no exact measurements.

Chocolate Ice Cream Bowls

◆ Melt 6 -1 ounce chocolate baking squares, according to package directions.

◆ Spread melted chocolate on cookie sheet, covered with wax paper.

◆ Blow up small round balloons to about 3-4 inches in diameter. Tie balloons to seal in air.

◆ Completely cover bottom two-thirds of balloons with melted chocolate. Use a spoon or paintbrush.

◆ Place chocolate-covered balloons in freezer for 5-10 minutes or set outside if it is wintertime!

◆ Use a straight pin to slowly release air from balloons. Carefully remove balloons from newly formed chocolate shells.

◆ Serve ice cream in chocolate bowls and enjoy! Serves 6.
  Note: Use dark or white chocolate, or a combination of the two.

Birthstones

Month	Birthstone
January	Garnet
February	Amethyst
March	Aquamarine
April	Diamond
May	Emerald
June	Pearl
July	Ruby
August	Peridot
September	Sapphire
October	Opal
November	Topaz
December	Turquoise

Birth Flowers

Month	Birth Flower
January	Carnation
February	Violet
March	Hyacinth
April	Sweet Pea
May	Lily of Valley
June	Rose
July	Delphinium
August	Gladiola
September	Aster
October	Marigold
November	Chrysanthemum
December	Narcissus

Resources

AARP Information Center
1503 W. 13th Street
Wilmington, DE 19806
302-656-2122
National newsletter, resources and information
for grandparents

American Bronzing
P.O. Box 6504
Columbus, OH 43209
1-800-423-5678
Baby shoe bronzing- call for brochure, pricing
and mailing bag

Boy's Life
P.O. Box 152079
Irving, TX 75015
Monthly magazine for boys ages 8 & up

Cookbook Publishers, Inc.
10800 Lakeview
Lenexa, KS 66061
1-800-227-7282
Personalized family reunion cookbooks

The Creative Grandparenting Newsletter
Creative Grandparenting
1503 W. 13th Street
Wilmington, DE 19086
302-656-2122
Quarterly newsletter for grandparents

Family Circle Magazine
1-800-627-4444
Monthly magazine for families

FamilyFun Magazine
1-800-289-4849
Monthly magazine for families

Family Ties
Individual Software, Inc.
5870 Stoneridge Drive #1
Pleasanton, CA 94588
1-800-822-3522
Easy-to-use, genealogy software program

full-time DADS©
P.O. Box 577
Cumberland Center, ME 04021
Bimonthly newsletter for dads

*Grandparent Power! How to Strengthen the
Vital Connection Among Grandparents,
Parents, and Children by Dr. Arthur Kornhaber*
Random House Books
400 Hahn Road
Westminster, MD 21157
1-800-733-3000
Book publishers

Grandparent Times
Caring Grandparents of America
400 Seventh Street NW, Suite 302
Washington, DC 20004-2206
202-783-0950
Membership and bimonthly newsletter for grandparents

Grandtravel
6900 Wisconsin Avenue, Suite 706
Chevy Chase, MD 20815
301-986-0790
Travel agency specializing in trips for grandparents and grandchildren

Helping Your Grandchildren Through Their Parents' Divorce by Joan Schrager Cohen
Walker & Co.
435 Hudson Street
New York, New York 10014
1-800-289-2553
Book publishers

Highlights for Children
P.O. Box 182348
Columbus, OH 43218
1-800-255-9517
Monthly magazine for children ages 4 & up

Ladybug Magazine®
P.O. Box 7434
Red Oak, IA 51591
1-800-827-0227
Monthly magazine for children ages 2-6
Also publish: Babybug: ages 6 mo.-2 (9 issues)
Spider: ages 6-9 and Cricket: ages 9 & up

Parents Magazine
1-800-727-3682
Monthly magazine for parents

Parrish and Brown Printing, Inc.
P.O. Box 1222
Wilkes-Barre, PA 18703
717-822-5033
Letters from the Easter Bunny, Santa Claus,
and Tooth Fairy

Reunions Magazine
P.O. Box 11727
Milwaukee, WI 53211
414-263-4567
Quarterly magazine for reunion planners

Safety For Toddlers®
31212 West Nine Drive
Laguna Niguel, CA 92677
Child Safety Consultants, send $2.00 for brochure. Inquire about local consultant and safety video.

Sports Illustrated for Kids
P.O. Box 83069
Birmingham, AL 35283
Monthly magazine for children ages 8-13

Stork News of America, Inc.
5075 Morgantown Road
Fayetteville, NC 28314
1-800-633-6395
Newborn announcement service- stork sign rentals

The Grandparent Gift Co., Inc.
707 Enterprise Drive
Westerville, OH 43081
1-800-4-MY-KIDS
Mail-order catalog, publishers

The Mommy Times®
P.O. Box 795
Balboa, CA 92661
1-800-99-MOMMY
http://www.mommytimes.com
National newsletter for moms

The Oppenheimer Toy Portfolio, Inc.
The Best TOYS, BOOKS & VIDEOS for Kids
40 East 9th Street
New York, NY 10003
212-598-0502
Annual book and quarterly consumer guide to
toys, books, videos, software and more

Together Time
The Creative Learning Institute
7 Indiana Hill Avenue
P.O. Box 208
Portland, CT 06480
860-342-3952
Monthly activity kits for parents and children

Your Big Backyard
8925 Leesburg Pike
Vienna, VA 22184
1-800-432-6564
Monthly magazine for children ages 3-5

Your Grandchild™
Trozzolo Resources Inc.
1102 Grand, 23rd Floor
Kansas City, MO 64106
1-800-243-5201
Bimonthly newsletter for grandparents

❖ ❖ ❖ ❖ ❖ ❖ ❖ Notes ❖ ❖ ❖ ❖ ❖ ❖ ❖

❖ ❖ ❖ ❖ ❖ ❖ ❖ Notes ❖ ❖ ❖ ❖ ❖ ❖ ❖